Borrowed Love Poems

Also by John Yau

100 More Jokes from The Book of The Dead (2001)
    (with Archie Rand)
Double-Headed Creature Features (2001)
    (with Max Gimblett and Tobin Hines)
My Heart Is That Eternal Rose Tattoo (2001)

Borrowed Love Poems

JOHN YAU

PENGUIN
POETS

PENGUIN BOOKS

Published by the Penguin Group
Penguin Putnam Inc., 375 Hudson Street,
New York, New York 10014, U.S.A.
Penguin Books Ltd, 80 Strand,
London WC2R 0RL, England
Penguin Books Australia Ltd, 250 Camberwell Road, Camberwell,
Victoria 3124, Australia
Penguin Books Canada Ltd, 10 Alcorn Avenue,
Toronto, Ontario, Canada M4V 3B2
Penguin Books India (P) Ltd, 11 Community Centre, Panchsheel Park,
New Delhi – 110 017, India
Penguin Books (N.Z.) Ltd, Cnr Rosedale and Airborne Roads, Albany,
Auckland, New Zealand
Penguin Books (South Africa) (Pty) Ltd, 24 Sturdee Avenue,
Rosebank, Johannesburg 2196, South Africa

Penguin Books Ltd, Registered Offices:
Harmondsworth, Middlesex, England

First published in Penguin Books 2002

1   3   5   7   9   10   8   6   4   2

LIBRARY OF CONGRESS CATALOGING IN PUBLICATION DATA
Yau, John, date.
Borrowed love poems / John Yau.
p.   cm.
ISBN 0-14-200051-5
I. Title.
PS3575.A9 B67 2002
811'.54—dc21   2001054864

Printed in the United States of America
Set in Bembo
Designed by M. Paul

for Eve now
and for Cerise Tzara when

What I am saying at this moment is not being said by me.
Osip Mandelstam

Acknowledgments

I am grateful to the editors and publishers of the magazines in which many of these poems first appeared: *American Poetry Review*; *Barrow Street*; *Boston Review*; *Conduit*; *Conjunctions*; *Denver Quarterly*; *First Intensity*; *Pierogi Press*; *Poetry Project Newsletter*; *Seneca Review*; *Tool*; *The World*.

Acknowledgment is also made to the following anthologies and editors: Rita Dove for selecting "Borrowed Love Poems" to appear in *Best American Poetry 2000* (series editor: David Lehman); Rosmarie Waldrop for including "Fifth Metabolic Isthmus Sestina" in the "Berlin Plus Portfolio" of *Exact Change Yearbook #1* (ed. Peter Gizzi and Exact Change) and for inviting me to contribute what became "the late tale" to *Reft and Light* by Ernst Jandl.

"I Was a Poet in the House of Frankenstein" was previously published by Tod Thilleman as a chapbook, *I Was a Poet in the House of Frankenstein* (MEB/PNY, 1999); "another late tale" previously appeared in *Reservations*, the catalog for an exhibition of Richard Tuttle at the BAWAG Foundation, Vienna, Austria; "storied fibs piled high" was previously published as *inside machine* with etchings by Hanns Schimansky and a CD by Peter Kowald (Editions Salzau, Germany, 2000); "Russian Letter (3)" was published as a broadside by the Dia Poetry Program, New York; "Russian Letter (6)" was previously published as *Letter from Marina* with woodcuts by Bodo Korsig (Editions Balance, Germany, 1999); the poems "Bowery Studio," "Studio Dream," "830 Fireplace Road," "830 Fireplace Road (2)," and "Broadcast from 791 Broadway" appeared, in earlier versions, in *New York Islands* with a drawing, lithographs, and photographs by Martin Nöel (Weidle Verlag, Germany, 1999); "Self-Portrait with Max Beckmann" was first published in *Berlin Diptychon* (Timken Publishers, New York, 1995).

Contents

Borrowed
Love Poems

I.

Russian Letter

It is said, the past
sticks to the present

like glue,
that we are flies

struggling to pull free
It is said, someone

cannot change
the clothes

in which
their soul

was born.
I, however,

would not
go so far

Nor am I Rembrandt,
master of the black

and green darkness,
the hawk's plumes

as it shrieks
down from the sky

Russian Letter (2)

Did we watch the phone sit still
like a frog

or did we dream of holding onto the flames
as they left this earth behind

Did we try to lead storm clouds
by their bridle

or did we toast the militant roses
as they marched toward the sun

Dear Cloakroom Granite
Dear Gunsmith's Notebook

crammed with watery receipts
Dear Conversation of Antennae

flickering in the shadows
huddled beneath a bridge

Did we let a few random phrases
haunt us

or did we mutter
about the dragonflies of death

Did you become a book I dreamed
or did I destroy

and contradict myself
like a moth

flying into language's
colorless flame

Russian Letter (3)

Dear Painter of Clouds
What proof will there be

after the shopkeeper
sweeps our dust into the gutter

And yet these moments are not
anyone's banner, not something

to be waved in the wind
sent aloft

a kite in the shape of a fish
vigorous sail above a winter beach

where we sit and watch
and walk

always back to our
separate rooms in the city

The fast full sky is not where we are swimming
if we are swimming at all

Dear Syllables Retrieved from the Rain
Dear Wind Alone with Your Song

Russian Letter (4)

Cara Finestra Aperta
Dear Mouth of Comets

Falling Through Your Hair
Dear Beginning of a Plural Blur

Mon Cheri
Muy Estimado

It was the year snow returned
to its original gray

Dear Zinc, Asphalt and Boatload of Rain
The sky's wall is rotting or blistered

peeling or toughened
shredded or stormed

Dear Lake of Missing Colors
It was the year smoke

turned its towers
from heaven to earth

Dear Occluded Light
or Black Oxidized Sand

Dear Sfumato Flower
Blooming in a Photograph

Are you a soft apparatus
a mechanical aid

for eye and hand
Dear Falling Butterfly

Dearest Wind-borne
Shadow of a Silhouette

Russian Letter (5)

Dear Bed of Snow,
do you still believe

there are people
who can inject happiness into every room

Dear Unrepayable Clock
when your eyes are charcoal

Is it a matter of gifts
thrown in the fire

for no other reason than to say
I like to sleep in a motel

I leave the other details of my existence
to doctors and watchmakers

Dear Masters of the Blinking Signs
who wants the last word

when so many
try to hide

their dead in ashes
their eyes like nails

ready to penetrate
the blackened earth

Russian Letter (6)

Amidst this haste and filth
beside the river's black violin

its sluggish summer tune
should I tell you how

you hide the dead
without singing

Dear Ungovernable Lament
Are you like a log

abandoned on a road of young trees
Or is your life a stone

smashed to
bits

About the one of yourself
and the one of the one

that is not you
but is the memory of what you wanted

I have only this to say
How is your life with an *image*

or has your memory started fading
until what you can pry loose

from the sea
is an island

etched in blue smoke
Dear Steam

How is your life with a stranger
from this world

the one we once walked in
argued over

and tried to burn

830 Fireplace Road

(Variations on a sentence by Jackson Pollock)

"When I am *in* my painting, I'm not aware of what I'm doing"
When aware of what I am in my painting, I'm not aware
When I am my painting, I'm not aware of what I am
When what, what when, what of, when in, I'm not painting my I
When painting, I am in what I'm doing, not doing what I am
When doing what I am, I'm not in my painting
When I am of my painting, I'm not aware of when, of what
Of what I'm doing, I am not aware, I'm painting
Of what, when, my, I, painting, in painting
When of, of what, in when, in what, painting
Not aware, not in, not of, not doing, I'm in my I
In my am, not am in my, not of when I am, of what
Painting "what" when I am, of when I am, doing, painting.
When painting, I'm not doing. I am in my doing. I am painting.

830 Fireplace Road (2)

No of the its of. Have the of have its
own have. Making have have.
No no because making changes
changes the making of the painting.
Image of have has its own no.
Image of no changes the because of painting.
No image because painting has a life of its own.
No "The" because life has a painting of its own,
its own image changes. Changes painting.
Image because the painting has.
Of making the image the because of painting,
of changes making the image the life of a painting,
I have no fear. Destroying the fear changes
the destroying I. I have no fear of destroying
the image of painting, no fear of making
no the because of painting,
of destroying painting. No, etc.
Painting. I have no fear of its image, its the.
I have no fear of destroying the no of painting,
the its of painting, the image of I.
Because of making, the I has no I.
Because changes because. I have no the.
Because the I has no image, no the, no its.
I have no fear of because,
no fear of destroying the I.
Destroying the because, the of, the etc.
No image of because, of its own, of has, of have.
Destroying the making of the I,
because the painting has no I of its own,
no no, no image, no the, no because of fear.
No image destroying changes, destroying the has.
Image of the I destroying image.

Image of fear making the image of I.
Image of life, its fear of its own.
I have the painting. The painting
has no I of its own. I have
no life. No image. No I I own.
Have I the painting? Have I the I of painting?
Of its because. Of its image. Of its fear.
The image changes, the painting has.
Making changes because,
the because of making changes.
The I of changes, the destroying I,
the its of the I. Because
the etc. has a life of its own, the changes.
I have no fear of destroying the image,
the painting, the changes, its the.
Changing the have, destroying the has.
The image of making fear change its life.
The image of the painting destroying the image.
The image of the I has a life of its own,
its own making, making the image of I.
I have no fear of destroying the image of making.
The image of I, the because of I.
I the painting destroying I the image,
making has has. Fear changes the destroying.
Destroying the fear, destroying the changes.
The destroying I of the image, the I of because.
I own no I. I own no painting.

Bowery Studio

It is never
just matter

Smooth as the paper
holding them in its mouth

the circles float
in their circles of ink

Solace is found in sameness
as is the soul

should one cling
to such matter

and such matters
mean much to some

But the sum
is not all

The circles float
in their perfect mouths of ink

Where else am I
to store them

The windows have their own tasks
The sky brings its own table

Studio Dream

Your face is a shoe
or a pyramid

What do you do
with a bandaged rock

clogged with muck
tea kettle's dented noggin

common clock
cracked with arrows

One is up or down
staring into book of stale bread

dotted slab and square cloud
Does the world move closer

when you scratch black lines
Bulb hangs its note above bed

Head and arms embrace dust
inside web

Did you want to join me on the sofa
watch my skull float out to sea

Old crust, stitched mitten
You've got a big empty head

but no place to cram it

Broadcast from 791 Broadway

Salacious, broken-nosed, bantamweight
Animals don't ring my doorbell
bring me cookies and champagne
biscuits as big as movie stars' post-nuptial crumbs
I am not another image of the Buddha preaching
or the ornate clouds he manufactures
for those in need of eternal wisdom
I am not even his rapid flagship cousin
part nugget, part fly
I am a defection from the mind of an
Abyssinian
tram
quill
rising through the pages of the wall
and wind you surround yourself in
almost hard-headed enough to make an appearance at the Statue
    of Librettists
because the Primogeniture Mink pleaded with me to grind for the
    people of New York
and to squirt you with news of how powerfully afloat we feel in
    Heaven
its many villas and huts copied from the terracotta model of
    Manhattan
we carried into the snowy mountains of thought

Since I left you, American art has received
many stamps and footnotes of approval
I was commissioned to design
by the School of Better Living Through Lusty Dancing and didn't

Since I left you, smoother stools and life-like
cats are being peddled by
the curlicue gates of the Museum of Modern Fate

Since I left you, well-groomed curators
have learned how to store their robes and purr
without becoming overly philosophical, and artists
have stopped skinny-dipping in the reflections
carried past their windows on the shoulders of dead and dying
    poets
disgusted perhaps by the sight of real flesh and blood

Since I left you, many other curious celebrations have taken place

Three Lullabies for Trakl

1.

The mountain named after the one
who stumbled into its shadow

The shadow made of slag and smoke
The mountain made of houses

where servants hang themselves
from the clouds

bunched beneath the rafters
The clouds made of houses

where children are sent to sleep
Are you at it again

The mountain dwindles when
another house

takes its place
No, that's not the name for it

Has the head floated off
dumping the body behind the bushes

Why do you call it a "house"
when no one lives there

One of us is walking out of the fire
One of us is pretending to sleep inside the smoke

House of smoke
House of fire

Are you at it again

2.

The moon stares into a mirror
A woman sees an empty dish

One animal licks another
Which of them is dead

I wrapped your scream in a star
I pinned two butterflies to its shadow

Why do we go on singing this song
when we know

all its words are nails
all our tongues pieces of wood

meant to build a house
for liars

The hills sink
beneath the rain

filling the cups
left out on the porch.

The hills we wanted to bury
behind the hills

so that we might weave
a hat or a hut

large enough for our friends
They were never our friends or yours

We do not know them any more
than we know these hills

One animal licks another
Why do we go on singing this song

3.

September hoists its flame against
brown and silver solid night

Did you ask yourself when
September bends its autumn fan

Houses extinguished
their dust let loose in the yard

September brushes rain from the pillow
Did you ask yourself when

the hair floated to the surface
Did you try and lift up its intolerant flame

Self-Portrait with Max Beckmann

One vision alone would be much simpler
but then it would not exist

Love in an animal sense is an illness
I am not a squirrel

though I have been told I eat like one
Everywhere attempts are being made

to lower our capacity for happiness
to the level of termites

To be sure, it is a foolish undertaking
to try and put ideas into words

Have you not sometimes been with me
in the deep hollow of a champagne glass

where red lobsters crawl around
and waiters serve flaming hats

mounted with pink and yellow flowers
Have you not given up searching

for a way out of the machine phantoms
Have you not observed the Law of the Surface

in the poisonous splendor of an orchid
Did you not set out to build a crystal hut

because you wanted to forge
three circles into a corner

Perhaps we will awaken one day
alone or together

Perhaps we will enjoy ourselves
in the forms we have been given

I am an acrobat climbing a ladder
a man in a tuxedo smoking a cigar

The clothes are a disguise
a small parcel I shall soon retract

To you
I am a not very nice man

who was lucky enough
to marry a beautiful woman from Graz

But to myself
I am a painter

who sleeps in a small room
adjacent to the long corridors

of a yellow night

Second Self-Portrait with Max Beckmann

I am falling into the harbor
carved out by Manhattan's skyscrapers

The pharaoh's boats quickly gather
at one end of the sky

Fire extends its many tentacles
through the clean office windows

Warmth fills the civic park
and with their short green wings

and thick violet tongues
climbing toward the sun

crowds of well-behaved tulips
mimic the flames

Fill up your mugs with beer
and hand the tallest one to me

Remember the song that begins
Stars are our eyes and nebulae our hair

Remember the benificent
effects of southern exposure

and the theory of meteors
that lets us sleep peacefully

I am trying to escape
the square on the hypotenuse

I am trying to reach the Hebrides
where a pink dress and black stockings

nestle themselves
close to you

amidst orchid blossoms
and clattering tambourines

Third Self-Portrait with Max Beckmann

I am incapable of writing to you
right now

Swarms of flies fill my room
as if it were an ant hill

and I am the last little bicycle
parked before the battlefront

II.

Movies as a Form of Reincarnation:
Boris Karloff Remembers Being Chinese on More Than One Occasion

1.

I was not born in Dulwich or Brighton, but in Camberwell, south London. Because I was illuminated from the outset, I did not find it necessary to become an animal, a water buffalo, a rat or a snake, in order to understand what Buddha was preaching. I did not even need to know such an immense figure might truly have existed, walking the bereft earth in a faraway place. This wasn't my job, which was easier than knowing. I didn't need to know, I only needed to pretend, become what you saw. Among pretenders, I was one of the best. So good in fact I have been confused with many of the shadows pinned against your city walls, embracing, as Walt Whitman did, the legions of castoffs, the hordes of those fate has tossed into the kegs. But Whitman could not make them walk the streets of your city as easily as I can. This is why I am still among you, a kind of peril whose color you might think you know, but are no longer so quick and willing to say.

2.

Time dissolves into drops suspended from a jagged black branch, my life. I will begin in the middle, working simultaneously toward both my demise and my birth, since they are the same moment. However, be duly forewarned about the use of such magic, as it can be tainted by those who try to bend it toward the cold caverns of the imagination, places where the light has been drained out of the jar, and only unidentifiable bones remain, like warning signals. Remember, only a movie actor can say these things without retribution, being as the body is not, as the audience has been fooled into thinking, a vehicle of the physical.

3.

A master thespian is never a vehicle, which, at best, is a wearisome form of servitude, something easily obtained and discarded. Rather, he or she is a librarian of the occult, a noble figure who accumulates a vast repertoire of irreplaceable motions and sounds. Because you thought I was given the key to that library, becoming in that regard its keeper, I was able to become a triumphant blur, an unmistakable hum in the night. These are the corridors where I wandered, a shrouded, lightning-haunted landscape at the edge of sight, a ruined world that memory, that deceiver, cannot shake loose. I tug at you when nothing and no one is there. I become what you see when you want to laugh or shudder or both, a clumsy oaf whose body, like a laboratory frog, twitches in time to the swaying violins and mournful trumpets, the knowing oboes.

4.

The story is simple because it is not a story, but a chain of events in which you are a link. One afternoon, in neither the distant future nor the nearby past, I happen to find myself confronted by a series of largely unspeakable circumstances, all of which were indelibly marked by the entrances and exits of my shadow. Thus, I am forced to quit my position at the White and Wong Detective Agency, and seek my fortune elsewhere.

5.

An itinerant detective and occasional time traveller, as all my kind are known to be, I learned various trades, all of which served me to become more and more distant from the one you thought was me. Among my accomplishments, I can list being handsomely rewarded for my sojourn in Black Castle, where I fed the alligators lolling in the manufactured mud. This was not all I pulled off in those years I strolled down Sunset Boulevard. During one particularly horrible Los Angeles summer, I was plucky enough to take up residence at Voodoo Island, where I became a gardener, and raised carnivorous

plants. Soon, however, I grew tired of fancy hotels, their bright lob-
bies and thick carpets. I wanted to penetrate the maze of corridors
intersecting the elevators, their ornate brass cages. It was time for
me to escape, to find refuge in a different form than the ones I had
so far been assigned. There were other bodies to be had, to have.

6.

Moments later, I departed the small fetching hamlet where I was
said to have been born, thrust into this world, I daresay, like a miser's
moonlit fist, embarking upon what I was sure was my journey to-
ward eternal redemption. How long was it before time began once
again to accelerate, its forehead beating the air, I do not know. All I
remember now is that at the first sign of dawn, and the ritual nail-
ing of the dove to a yellow cloud, I beat a tactical but hasty retreat
into the forest the gods had so handily dropped beside a lake, not
far from the Dew Drop Inn, where two men and a horse had gath-
ered to discuss the recent hijacking of the president's substitute
body. It was this body, rather than his own, that they wanted to in-
stall in a museum, sure that it would attract the curious and the
morbid, the tearful and those seeking further proof of the miracu-
lous. I, however, was not satisfied with being esconced in a mu-
seum. My body, I proclaimed to the sky, was not to be fitted so
easily into a display case.

7.

Although the future had not yet vomited anywhere near where
I had stopped to survey my own increasingly meager options, it
wasn't long before I learned that my own body was to endure a
plight similiar to that of the president's doppelganger, his hired
dummy. Thus, after a fortnight of munching on acorns in a tangled
black mass of thorns and branches, cold sunlight finally saw fit to
stir me from my humble stupor. It was in this potentially embarrass-
ing situation, muddy and covered with manufactured cow manure,
that I discovered what I hoped was not my final fate: I had become

a half-wit servant. Even worse, some unthinking, uncaring parent, who I would never know, much less have the chance to throttle, had forever cursed me with the name of Voltan. Even the villagers were quick to point out that it sounded like a dented car whenever I stumbled into a room and began mumbling before them, the bowl of my large empty hat waiting to be filled with whatever curses fell that day from the ceiling or sky.

8.

I tried to tell them that my real name was Mr. Wong, that for many years I had been gainfully employed as a detective, and that both my peers and my enemies believed me to be blessed with a third eye, an inner oculus. I was, I repeatedly told them, famous for my ability to pass as someone else. Had they not heard of the bandit Fang, who alone among thieves was a principled man doomed to die and be reborn as the frightening, though short-lived "Invisible Menace"? So many adventures, none of which seemed to have ever been transcribed in the official records, much less remembered by the occupants of this isolated village. Had they not seen me before, many times in fact? Why don't they know who I am? They think of me as an idiot, a fool, some disheveled thing rather than one of them. And when they tilt toward me, act as if attention is all they possess, my life story is but an interlude, a moment in which to slap the table and howl. It is time to mimic my every gesture, to repeat my every halting word. I have become the shadow they shadow, that is their daily delight.

9.

How could they not know that I had once been a shadow that pulled the gestures of others back, until they became mine. In such a manner, I had passed time as an ex-con and a spiritualist, a spy and a surgeon. In each life I lived, the mask I wore was my own face. It resembled your dreams of how such a face should look when peering through a torn curtain, a fogged-over windshield, a martini glass filled with blood. It was a face you knew because you knew the outcome. This was how I was able to become Chinese so often, more times than anyone else who set out from a town or village, toward the paved driveways and marble bathrooms of Pacific Palisades.

10.

My dream was simple; to be ensconced in fur, to loll like a seal, to dream with my eyes open. Today, sitting at my desk, writing this memoir, at last I am able to ask: Was this not how Fu Manchu and Frankenstein were born? Didn't you, dear reader, dear viewer, not already dream of them before they were ever known to cast their shadows across humanity's noble visage? Did you not predict that they would stalk the earth, wreak havoc, cause untold misery, be caught and finally destroyed, their mortal bodies plunged at last into the spiritual fires?

11.

Isn't it true that you did not need to see my face to know it was me swathed in dusty bandages? that it was me rising from the Horus-headed coffin locked in a secret chamber deep inside the pyramid? Didn't you already know that only I could possess the formula necessary to transmit my body, its blur, across and through time? Isn't it me that you've been waiting for all along, as if I am a messiah, a lover, and an enemy all rolled into one hideous corpse? And if, for the next few hours, you sit before the flickering screen, waiting for my face to finally be uncovered, so that at last you can see my jutting jaw and sallow cheeks, my high, unforgettable forehead and large ears, all the while reveling in my thick-tongued speech bordering on a hideous lisp, it is so you can get up and walk away, open the refrigerator or look in the mirror, glad that you have been right all along.

12.

Finally, you think, such perfection doesn't belong to me, but to you. It is why I have been placed before you, both as a warning and as something to remember. A talisman you slip back in your pocket, a coin whose face has been eroded by years of unthinking caresses, something spent in a moment dedicated to frivolity. Am I each of these or none? Or am I what vanishes behind your eyes without ever going away?

Genghis Chan: Private Eye XXIX

(Fourteen Ink Drawings)

Mirror   film   stain
Gown   tiger   glass
Canopy   powder   bell
Mulberry   blister   festival
Boat   portrait   box
Vermillion   chestnut   cloud
Milk   shadow   moon
Breeze   identical   face
Ink   ladder   jar
Orchid   chimney   tongue
Parachute   sword   wave
Groom   motel   coffee
Anvil   clock   hair
Condom   audience   dog

Genghis Chan: Private Eye XXX

shoo war
torn talk

ping towel
pong toy

salted sap
yellow credit

hubba doggo
bubba patootie

wig maw
mustard tongue

Peter Lorre Reminisces About Being a Sidekick

Iron cloud, bronzed sunset, stolen dream.
I wasn't always a feverish lepidopterist
chasing whistling chariots in a stadium.
My wax lacked coherence, my human hairs glistened.
Perhaps you would like to come in off the ledge
and share a mug of hot cocoa laced with absinthe.
Or is that the kind of little naughtiness you prefer to shun?
Have you noticed that there's a lot of snow
clinging to my last Fabergé egg?
Take off your tie, throw away your shoes.
Have you seen my collection of portholes?
some pried from the very finest luxury liners
to have foundered on these rocky shores.
It's not that I am given to issuing a high-resolution
lightly thawed whoop or two
whenever my oversized eyelids
belly fat knuckles start twittering,
and the crease in my gabardines start gabbing
to the pleats gathered at the corner, waiting
for the light to change its spots,
but I just love yodeling
"O sweet spotless tyrannosaurus,
why hast thou huffiness handcuffed me
to the Hunting Lodge of Unrepentant Nations
and their sprawling kin? Am I not
allowed a few extra paces
before I am commanded
to run into the woods?"
Such timely intermissions prove
how newly minted and hot I became,
while sitting on a painted horse,
surrounded by dancing dandelions.

Did I forget to mention the adventures of Smoky Muskrat,
Maison Spittle, and Cheap Varmint Night and his Band,
The Sheep Bladder Brigade? Or am I being too allegorical,
too much a one night pill flipper in a copycat's storm?
Will I ever be regarded as truly satisfying?
Can I become one who exudes
a heroic magnetic profile?
become one whose blessed visage pulls the dust
off your brow of well-endowed verbs?
Will you remember me as something more
than an imported bandana
when I am draped in bad blood squirted from a can
made of recycled helmets retired ogres pitched in a ditch?
Hey, are you glugging to the ghosts of Salvation Coliseum?
This isn't a resurrection factory, you simian of slime.
What are you doing? walking your toast
down to the coroner's barn? Quit hawking
your perforated hanky, there is always more of this
where this came from. Remember, the last time
you had your brain amputated, you were required
to sacrifice your definitions of meandering reincarnations
in favor of a satchel of bologna pizzas.
Or were you just another hungry artist
quick to lick the trumpet of integrity?
Hard to dream about the outside when it stops
raining long enough to forget you once had
a memorable name. This is where I get off
the bus, Buster. Or is it Bruiser or Boozer,
Flappy or Winsome with an Axe?
On the other side of the lake lives a two-headed dragon.
Pink smoke rises from the nostrils of the one known
as Ying, while blue tears fall from the one known as Yank.
It is rumored that they used to be Siamese twins
but got tired of eating from the same hollywood bowl.

As a dishwasher, I became familiar with their plight,
and tried to comfort them, but with little consequence.
You encounter all sorts of shadows in this game preserve.
Some have been suspended in the trees for eons,
their souls locked inside the recyclable peanut
butter jars insulating the wizard's hexagonal library.
That's how I plan to get promoted to Senior Gatekeeper.
A small wagon floated downstream, guided by nymphs.
Huge fragrant bouquets descended from the rafters,
quickly covering the stage, but, by then,
the headline star had fled into the closet
the management rented out for such occasions.
Time to hoist your mortal spoils out of bed, Bunky.
I wasn't trying to become you when the mountain
tugged itself together, collapsing outside the doghouse
where I pass my afternoons, dreaming of the day
my portrait will finally hang in the dog museum.
You pass more than afternoons, you blasphemous pustule
on the noble edifices that have been studiously erected
by a fleet of robots, sleek and newly released,
like a certain frog's vivacious belch, from
the recently upgraded prison recreation facility
just down the road from the gas station where I saw you
licking grease off the monkey they keep
tucked behind the cash register.
I wasn't always this gentle. In fact,
I wasn't always an Austro-Hungarian umpire, either.
Twice I've been from somewhere
outside your sovereignty. Once I was even Japanese,
but that was before the war brought us home,
to the blue picket fence draped with ribbons and razors.
Quit smooching the mirror, goggle-eyes. You got a face
that could pass as a kangaroo's pouch.
Not that I don't muster up some small careful affection

for that doomed race of puddle hoppers,
but we all jump into oblivion, don't we?
Maybe you ought to get into another line of work.
Maybe you ought to fold your name somewhere else,
sign on someone else's dotted line
since you were never issued one in the first place.
I am sure I can find you an envelope big enough.
What about the barrel of forks you hid in the alley?
Say, what are you doing here anyway?
Who said you could stop by and smear lemon grass
meringue over your cloudy lapels? You think
you got something big to say? Something momentous?
Or is it what you had to memorize
in order to escape the men with lightning in their eyes?

Boris Karloff in *The Mummy Meets Dr. Fu Manchu*

Emerging from the woods, the audience stumbles upon an isolated scene: In the late afternoon's arcade of artificial gloom, a dainty, dotted hand deftly smooths the lower slope of a massive forehead. Zoom to close-up: Thick oblong plane's corrugated surface, its vertical grooves sprouting with stiff thistle or hard clumps of new hair. Moving suddenly into focus is a multi-leveled chorus of angular limbs festooned with pin-pricked skulls of uncategorizable animals. A paleontological nightmare thinks the perverse paleontologist, her imported platinum tongue stud momentarily glistening between her lover's neatly pointed teeth. Color-coded keys shift and finally settle at bottom of lint-lined pocket. Sharks churn and chug, excited by the array of scents swiftly filtering through their olfactory detectors. Defined by the lingering traces of a mischievous grin, one that suggests satisfaction of a nonverbal order, a heavily jacketed though unpimpled boy points out the newly severed head of the evening moon, which, elsewhere, is floating directly above the Bank of Shanghai's misaligned ideograms and misplaced radicals.

Soon, every member of this roped-off section of time and space will meld into the unnumbered ranks of invisible spectators condemned to wander across the inclines of a barnacle-encrusted city. Gladys tugs at her store-bought underwear. Is the name of its color forget-me-not?

For a month of free parking, you must answer the following question: Whose gloved digits parted the black petals of the actress's accordion before the votive candles slid out of view?

She hears but cannot determine the origin of a voice which whispers, you are guilty of secreting liquids of a private nature into the public basement.

A nameless place in the universe or a dead phase in a mechanized elephant's recently restored memory bank, no one knows.

In the lower balcony, Jiminy Jimmy tries not to muffle the bundle of fidgeting taking up space beside him. He dreams of the day he can leave his insect self behind, a papery husk gathering human dust in the shallow valley of a velvet cushion. Outside, beneath the curtains of the evening sky, the mournful cries of a disgruntled tyrant are quickly punctuated with the boiled dust of his headless ancestors. Rows of soldered bells and newly unfolded buses are waiting to absorb the growing stream of visitors. On the screen, hordes of infected termites eat through the edges of the unfurling role-call. A large gathering of beady eyes begins investigating the remains of this tiniest of essays.

Night's panorama of stars is no longer a coming attraction.

Hans Violin enters the tunnel and emerges as Hank Harmonica, bit player and familiar television talk show guest. Meanwhile, after waking up in another section of the numbered quadrant, Gus "The Big" Viola discovers he has been reduced to a small-boned, foreign-born dry cleaner. Time briefly accelerates its production of contaminated images. Realizing that, while he will always remain foreign to those who seek the indelible signature of his services, he has unwittingly let himself succumb to a flurry of mispronunciations. In doing so, he has become an even smaller, small-boned servicer of others. However, now no longer either a dry or clean specimen, Gus decides he must lessen the flow of his daily sobbing. Otherwise, he is incapable of eliminating his love of operatic presentation, even though fate is about to cast him as a person without merit, a clod or a heel, a snippet of abject flotsam inhabiting a zone fit for exhaust fumes and unapologetic vandals. What he doesn't yet know, but which the audience suspects, is that his tears, however few may fall, will slowly stop evaporating.

Bones and cars accumulate at the bottom of the lake.

Without knowing exactly why—he is in this regard still optimistic about the future—Gus begins wishing he was wearing a red leather poncho and sitting at a shiny black piano. Somewhere in the back of the spacious, aromatic auditorium, a young woman clutches a tattered plastic rose to the tattooed Turkish dagger above her quickly beating heart. She feels the beads of sweat tightening around Gus's long, slender neck. He has become a swan pedaling around a small lake surrounded by tanks. It is winter and the war is in its sixty-fifth year. The large, antiquated camera swivels haphazardly toward the next set of sprockets. A speck becomes a many-legged shadow hovering above a roofless manger, where a one-eyed mother comforts her two-headed infant. The audience gasps; it is the only acceptable response a civilized person can make under the circumstances.

As we are unable to escape the law of averages, there is, of course, one exception. You see, I have entered your line of sight, a tall, almost shapeless profile with long arms, hands, and fingers stiffly extended, as if, of their own accord, they are searching for some malleable form to embrace and squeeze.

I am swathed in thick, wide bandages, which makes it difficult to offer a newly minted hanky to Gus, the tear-stained dry cleaner, who ignores the puddle slowly forming by his feet. I am standing in his store or, as the blue lettered sign on the window states, his very reliable and friendly establishment. Was I drawn here because he too is foreign? an impediment to speech? Did he exude a magnetic field I could not veer away from? Was this collision planned by large unseen forces known to move in mysterious ways?

My sole purpose is to inquire how I might go about finding someone who can aid me. The goal was stated at the outset by my pharaoh father, before the first effects of his second reincarnation set in: I am to find my original identity, the one from which I and my sperm bank embarked, many eons ago. Not the one Gus sees before him, wrapped in dusty bandages, but the one inhabiting the one whose face is covered with strips of cloth soaked in the Nile.

The sky darkens to the color of a bruise and the last of the renegade stars are quickly nailed into place.

It is a silly thing, to ask someone how you might go about finding out who you are. Presumably you already know. But, in my case, I am of two minds and at least two bodies. One is only visible to me. The other is the one I inhabit but cannot catch sight of.

My dilemma is familiar. I can't recognize my reflection, as I can only nod to the shadows the director has painted on the wall behind me. These painted blobs move in tandem to my hesitations. We could begin to dance, but that would only prove a distraction to those whose attention I have gathered like wool on a spring day.

Oh ferry man, perhaps I too was meant to guide puppets across the River Styx.

Certainly, my mission, if you can still call it that, remains largely unknown to me, the dry cleaner, and the audience. The small glances cannot be strung together. Rather, we manage to form the extendable legs of a polished aluminum tripod, on top of which someone has installed a motorized camera. All the seats are taken; and there is nowhere else to move. Time to hunker down and look forward. Darkness, it seems, is approaching, a swift car galloping majestically across the diamond red tundra. As advertised in the brochure, the temperature is starting to plummet. In the short time you have left, you must persuade the couple in front of you to remove their hats and wigs.

After *My Chronology* by Peter Lorre

The splattered flag of an idiot scavenger; this was how
I sailed beyond the perfect faces of the coming storm.
Many times, almost as many as in your shabby arenas,
their walls of baritone shadows, their stream of flailing ants.
I was rolled beneath a couch. Stuffed in a trunk. Drooled
down a box (complete with fishing tackle,
their silvery tangle and heap of pink wigglers).
Flopped into a crumpled cup. A semi-anonymous heap.
Shorn of all but secondary features, some of which
were legendary, petals of manufactured smoke
erasing butterflies shivering in the branches of my material
    remains.
Did you try and insert me in a pile of juggled lumps?
Was I part of a column of figures? Or was I
a figural column surrendering sky's black roof?
Who traces the umbilicus of these outbursts of frenzy
back to its mouth, my carriage of sagging carbon
cries out? Who embraces these hummingbird sparks of lateral
    agitation?
A monogrammed hanky steeped in sepulchral vapors?
Pathetic this monaural chivalry.

Once I even crawled around a lake resting in
the crevice of a porcelain saucer, before being
swatted into diaphanous mulch, leaving only
an inky signature on the lard inflated plains.
What is chronology, but detachable hands
sifting for condensation collectivized in an earlier era?
Could I not have arrived before you opened your eyes,
found your axial culmination seated in the upper registers
of a Babylonian balcony or Sumerian wing chair,
optically registering disturbances flooding through

the illuminated window? Or were you always there,
always perfectly poised, stored among the glass roses
you will be requested to accompany to the heated antechamber?
Always waiting for the mirror to begin reciting the contents of its
    solid lake?

I Was a Poet in the House of Frankenstein

Do you remember me as a spy
in a mythical European kingdom?
How about when I am a French Canadian trapper?
a role I play a number of times.
I kidnap Henrietta Barge. It isn't the last time
I will commit such a dastardly act.
I belong to a band of marauders
presided over by the evil Mangua,
played by Wallace Beery.
I am the villain Ahmed Khan
and a villainous halfbreed
who abducts the heroine in a canoe.
The ruler of a fictitious Menang Island,
I order the wholesale massacre of the white settlers.
I live in Old Baghdad and make tents.
I become a maharajah and, once again,
I am a French Canadian trapper.
A Mexican halfbreed, a mate
on a rum smuggling ship,
an evil governor:
I am each of them and more.
During World War I, I am a scissors grinder in Vienna.
Both earlier and later, depending on the way
you tell time, I am a scurvy-looking
crew member of the pirate Jean Lafitte.
I continue being a Barbary pirate.
I am a deserving victim in a murder mystery.
My name is Blackie Blanchette: I rob railroads.
This is my card: Snipe Collins, fiendish crook.
I live among lion worshippers.
Usually, I am one of the main villains.
I disinter, smuggle, conspire,

I behead, betray, swallow,
I shoot, throttle, gasp.
I am the ship's purser.
I live in swashbuckling New Orleans;
my name is Fleming.
The Vanishing Rider,
Vultures of the Sea.
In *Burning the Wind,*
I am a wicked ranch foreman
who carries off the heroine.
Hoot Gibson is the good guy.
I am Maurice Kent,
stewing in a cabin in the "northwoods."
Small furry animals are part of the plot.
I once played a man named "Boris."
I am a henchman, call me Cecil.
In the Charlie Chan murder mystery
Behind That Curtain,
my name is "Karlov."
The first time I spoke on screen,
I was a Hindu servant.
The director of the film was Lionel Barrymore.
Instead of being the villain,
as everyone thought,
I am the heroine's father.
I am a prison guard.
My boss is a sadistic overseer.
I star in *Sea Bat.*
Charles Bickford
manages to escape
Devil's Island.
I play a villainous sheik
with a phony French accent
in a film about a young American

who escapes from an Indian prison.
I am a "trusty" who kills a "stool pigeon."
I become a revolutionary
in the kingdom of El Dorania.
I sell dope, the stronger the better.
I am a crooked gambler
who tries to cheat a barber.
I am a crook's cultured accomplice.
Will Rogers is a razorblade king from Oklahoma,
I am a sheik.
I work as a butler.
I am an unscrupulous newspaper
editor's evil assistant.
A clubfoot man
who loves to dance,
I teach my son, Fedor,
who, of course, becomes famous
making me happy, scared, and jealous.
A madman kills me during the performance of a ballet.
I am a gangster, a beer baron.
I work as Lionel Barrymore's orderly.
I try to hide on a yacht, but I am caught.
I am on the dirigible *Los Angeles,*
exploring the South Pole.
Many members of the team,
myself included, perish.
I am on the lam,
I hide, shiver, moan, and grunt.
I play the part of a prison warden,
and then I am lying on a table in a castle,
waiting to be born.
My name is Frankenstein,
and I am deathly afraid of fire.
I manage to become a waiter.

I work as an autopsy surgeon,
and I am malevolent.
I play myself, eating in a well-known restaurant.
My name is Nikko; I am a charlatan.
I pretend to be a faith healer.
I direct a narcotics ring.
In ancient Egypt,
I am a prince
who breaks into the tomb
where the princess I love
has been buried.
A brutish dumb
but homicidal butler.
I own a nightclub,
and wear no makeup.
I steal the mask of Genghis Khan
from the British Museum
in an attempt to start a "holy war."
I am Dr. Fu Manchu,
both Chinese and sinister.
A torturer of the innocent.
I am both
a half-mad recluse
and a master criminal.
After I am buried alive,
I return to claim
a priceless jewel
which someone has stolen from me.
Lon Chaney, Bela Lugosi, and I
appear in a cartoon.
I am the evil host.
Bela Lugosi is the sinister stranger.
The movie is *House of Doom*
directed by Edgar G. Ulmer,

who, because of the Nazis,
was forced to flee Germany.
I am an insane religious fanatic,
trying to incite my people
to destroy a British patrol
which has gotten lost in Mesopotamia.
As the anti-Semitic Baron Ledrantz,
I try to destroy the House of Rothschild.
I am able to transfer
all my thoughts and feelings
into someone else.
I am "Dr. Maniac, the brainsnatcher."
In *Charlie Chan at the Opera,*
I am Gravelle, a former baritone
possessed by homicidal tendencies.
After Charlie Chan cures me of my insanity,
I resume my career in the opera.
While engaged, with my partner
Bela Lugosi, in astronomical research
in Africa, I am contaminated
by a radioactive meteorite.
Anyone I touch dies.
I try to kill Lugosi
because he wants to stop me
from killing Frank Lawton,
who is having an affair with my wife.
In the story of the man
who is brought back to life
after he is electrocuted,
I am wrongly accused of murder
and put to death.
I return, a strange, remote, possessed,
and obsessed being,
completely animated

by one idea: revenge.
My name is Mallory;
I invented a burglar alarm,
which was stolen from me
by Ranger. Twenty years
have passed and I am
about to go blind.
But, before I do,
I invent an invisible ray system
which enables me to silence
my foolproof burglar alarm.
In 1937, in the northern oilfields of China,
I am the Chinese bandit Fang,
a good guy who dies because of his beliefs.
In 1938, in San Francisco,
I am Mr. Wong,
an unassuming but meticulous
specialist in crime investigation.
Because I help
a wounded, escaped prisoner,
I am sentenced to Devil's Island for treason.
My name is Doctor Gaudet.
Edwards, a collector of jewels and antiques,
gains illegal possession of the gem,
"Eyes of the Moon," which was seized
from the Nanking Museum during a riot.
When he is murdered
during a game of charades,
I decide to track down the murderer.
My name is Mr. Wong.
In *Mr. Wong in Chinatown,*
my name is Detective James Lee Wong.
Princess Lin Haw, played
by Lotus Long, is murdered

by a dart from a bamboo tube
hidden inside a sleeve, a weapon
well known to the Chinese
and those familiar with their ways.
The story centers around
a "mechanical" heart
that restores life to the dead,
but changes the whole
character of the revived man.
Baron Wolf von Frankenstein
returns to the castle
where he discovers I am in a coma,
tended to by a crazy shepherd.
I am the grim clubfoot executioner, Mord.
Captain Street's best friend,
Detective O'Grady, is murdered
and I am called in to solve the case.
This is the fourth time I am Mr. Wong,
but the sixth time I am Chinese.
I have not yet added up the times
I am less than human, a halfwit,
a necrophiliac, or a ghoul.
I am an absentminded
professor of English literature,
who is run down in the street.
In order to save me,
part of a dead gangster's brain
is transplanted into my skull.
I dress as an ape, and obtain
the liquid needed for the serum.
I am the German ace-spy, Strendler.
I invent a machine which can communicate with the dead.
I steal the body of a woman from a newly dug grave.
I am a Greek general in the Balkan War

visiting the island where my wife was buried fifteen years ago.
I escape from prison.
I am the head of an insane asylum known as Bedlam,
and I have a mistress who will turn against me.
I am a crazed clothes designer.
My name is Gruesome, and Dick Tracy
will throw me in the clink.
My name is Guyasuta, Chief of the Senecas.
I am Tishomingo, a friendly, educated Choctaw.
I am Mr. Hyde.
I am the ferocious
head of a band of dope smugglers
on the island of Ischia.
I work as the local rajah's military chief.
I am Baron Victor von Frankenstein, the last of my family.
I am a novelist investigating a gruesome murder,
two decades old, which,
in another personality, I committed.
I am a doctor during the early days of anaesthesia.
I am a wicked wizard living in a slimy green castle.
My archenemy, another sorcerer, is Vincent Price.
During the prologue, he reads
Edgar Allan Poe's poem "The Raven."
I am a necrophiliac baron
intent on preserving my dead wife.
Jack Nicholson tries to rescue her,
but ends up with her turning to dust in his arms.
My co-stars are Vincent Price and Peter Lorre.
I am Amos Hinchley, Price's senile father-in-law.
I am an East European vampire who carries
someone's head in a sack.
One day, I tear out the throat of my four-year-old grandson.
I walk on *Bikini Beach*.
I have the voice of a rat.

I am a blind sculptor.
I cannot see the ghost in the invisible bikini.
I am bearded, I limp.
I start out ordinary, kind,
but end up a hideous monster.
My job is to reenact the role of a mad scientist.
I am Professor Marsh, witchcraft expert.
I am Byron Orlok, an aging actor
who became famous for his horror roles.
I want to retire.
A young married man
with an obsession for guns
decides to kill me.
He sees me once,
through a telescopic lens,
and then in two places.
I am on the screen of a drive-in movie,
where he has come with his rifle,
to kill more innocent bystanders,
and I am walking toward him,
an aged but determined man with a cane.

Film Adaptations of Five of America's Most Beloved Poems

It burns and winds. For as long as I can remember, my Sunday task has been to polish the antique wooden perambulator until it gleams like an aluminum bread box. Do you mind being the landlady's favorite pet? No, Little Igor, raunchy ruminator and muralist to mid-sized manufacturers, these are not the horoscope dials you should be consulting. Look at the fuzzy ones over there, on the pink control panel mounted beneath the custom aquarium populated with poisonous snakes, addled alligators, and small but hearty fish. Have you ever seen such a diverse array of live entertainment clouding the waters before?

On misty days the sun hangs pale blue over a black diamond sea. Academic painters of every persuasion rise from their imported beach chairs and press their ointment-covered noses against the unnecessarily spotted glass, unaware that cross-eyed snakes are staring back at them. Intrepid mountaineers follow the whistle of the marmot up to the highest crags, and over playgrounds and puddles alike rises the cry of a wounded sea otter, fondling the most delectable portion of his imported fish dinner. Meanwhile, a caravan of carrion has been dragged across the sand.

It turns and whines. All motels are penetrated by two sounds—a scream and a complaint. Today, as long ago, these are the two sacred messengers of the Western Nile Plumbers' Union and their far-flung subsidiary units. Trying to overcome the image of being nothing more than a bunch of loud-talking, gum-chewing cronies, the union leaders decided to dispense with opening ceremonies and closing sermons. Later, concerned with the rank-and-file's growing resentment of enforced civic duty, some of the leaders voted to reenact well-known gaffes at previous company picnics, while others elected to learn the intricacies of miniature collie and poodle grooming as an alternative to hosting the Sunday car wash. Their favorite costumes included a red satin tuxedo, a cowboy moustache, and nicotine-stained talons. Last month, the duly elected Vice-Secretary issued the following decree: No velvet cones with tassels are allowed to cross the threshold.

High above the Wabash River, its riverbanks lined with quaint cobblestone streets and newly renovated factories, complete with working fire hydrants and helmeted dwarfs scattered discreetly among the hordes of wayward children, a foreign possibly alien power has managed to thrust the city's entire workforce into a state of suspended animation. The mayor fears the immense stone bridge that was to become a major tourist attraction in the tri-county area will remain unfinished. The pianist is trying to imitate the sound of an oncoming train. No one dreams that the images are stolen from a semi-retired sorcerer while he is dreaming of a miniaturized sorcerer who is assassinated and buried in a jelly jar by a quartet of indignant barbers. A hexagonal shield gleams in the ruby-colored gloom descending from the sky. Great ospreys nest in the crowns of the unfinished arches. Four goats wander across the ice. The head goat, William of Upper Broadway, keeps reminding Thutmoss of the likelihood that strange plants are migrating rapidly across the ocean floor.

A man pleads with the creature locked inside an imported hair dryer to reconsider the wording of their oath. The less said about the source of this rumor, the better. After taking refuge in a deserted gas station containing seven slim coffins, one for each gambling centipede, the high-brow hero—he has a forehead the size of Rhode Island—decides to return from hell to find out why his latest girlfriend didn't follow him to the very ends of the earth. Meanwhile, in a drugstore in Angela, Ohio, an attractive young woman by the name of Akron decides to buy two lottery tickets, one for each side of the coin.

Peter Lorre Records His Favorite Walt Whitman Poem for Posterity

I am an indigestable vapor rising from the dictionary
you sweep under your embroidered pillow

My only offer: A kidnapped dog in exchange for your thirst
Call me Zanzibar Sam, Bulging Pharaoh, Narcoleptic Swill

Custom labyrinths made to order, purveyor of mid-sized jungles
a gravedigger counting shoes in a candlelit saloon

A miracle erupted from a reunion of mouse and sow, horse and
    hubby
Son became bagged contraband penetrating ring of nibbled pyres

Me criminal puss no longer muzzled and mugged by snoring
    camera
Me signaled pasty or patsy, but donned smooth glacial twitches

Mere slip in a sequined slapper, lolling whimper of purring grape,
not just smoothed flotsam bulk and hankering moss

Inside me dwells a nude drummer toy, all pomade and fancy,
while the outer me, the bun you tufted, was heavy-lipped

reflection of uncanny twittering amidst gnawed leaves

Peter Lorre Speaks to the Spirit of Edgar Allan Poe During a Séance

Back then which is anywhere in back of now
I was pretending to be a practicing mendicant

a mower of smaller children, a moratorium in a tuxedo
while you were acting like a hopeless sponge

a photograph of a convict whose mind
isn't quite made up, but it is

Later, I draped the last of my outer garments
over my jockey shorts, and left town in a cab

I told the man whose shiny head
reminded me of a bottle of wine

Deliver me to the suburban rodeos of
Piccadilly or Paradise

a harbor of idle tugboats
an island of glass huts

wherever smoke hasn't started
charting its progress across a shorn sky

Thus, the journal of our journey
and the urinal of our yearning

began with the opening of faucets;
tear ducts; syrupy vittles;

Arctic ice storms; bowler hats
above long thick sleeves;

white-haired gymnasts and their smelly pets
The detectives came later

examples of their tarnished industriousness
tucked beneath their pressed pink tongues

Did you know that I was never called upon
by those who would have known

what I meant
when I said

I was a star
in an early

stage of deterioration
a page upon which

someone has drawn
the seven shapes of my name

their skeletal facades
pressing against deserted streets

The rest of me—the part you know
as it is also you—

is sitting inside a bus station
watching television,

waiting for further instructions on how
I might dig myself out of the roles

blind biographers have stuck me in

III.

Things I Should Tell You Before It's Too Late

Princess Sitting Duck isn't my real name
I am not one of the ones marred

by inexplicable outbursts of an obstreperous nature
Most times I'm a curtain of conviviality

Don't make friends with my dog
I used to collect ideas until I realized

I don't have any of my own
Learn to shirk your duties

with dignity I always say
I used to dress in a squirrel suit

and play in the forest
where it flanks the railroad tracks

leading to the haunted mines
I never reached the rank of colonel

You can hold my hand
as long as you don't lose it

I serve drinks in tall blue glasses
I am never sure which principles are mine

Sometimes I get glassy-eyed
and pee on the neighbor's porch

I no longer throw stones at children
I bow whenever I see a high-ranking dignitary

stop to ties his shoes
or zip up his fly

Princess Sitting Duck isn't my nickname either

Didn't They Like You as Much as They Like Themselves?

Whenever I am
humanity's defecation
being an old
cafeteria dog
said detonation dan
a trampled pimple
in double feature
panoramic head
never properly
doomed
or groomed
when
I begin
coughing flies
a little toy
coffee cup
ladled with lava
catches when voices said
you can't squeeze
ketchup from a turnip
you just burn up
no can catch up
when you turn up
said wind squeezes
remote control
widow into corner
I said wings rust
a bird red as clouds
suspended in glass
said ones in head
would migrate

to another station
south of anchor
and seersucker
where a blue taxi
(always only one)
pulls its pearls
across evening sky
while many
(this too is true)
different shaped couples
flit about
scooping up tears
some shinier
others not so
they said I was spooned
to wrong stationary object
said I said voices
in heads are never tuned
too open and yellow
to be the sun
bearing its flashlight
down on us bugs
I am a many-legged projectile
flopping into the fire
said voices under broad
brow of borrowed car
its glass forehead
shattered by arteries
slipping out of their harnesses
the kind of strength
you need voices in your head
to turn the tune
back to its extinction
is a kind of paralegal imprisonment

one never escapes ice or its house
frozen in a reflection that never blurs
said voices said ones in elevator's brain
would stop transmitting birdcalls to worms
voices said voices in head would better
breathe itself into an ant castle
said beetles carry voice's imprint
on their dotted shells
said I heard myself
talking to you when I was you

Retired Wrestler

Usually, when the late-afternoon sun
thickens, and battle-weary clouds

begin resembling recycled bandages
I prepare to hop out on the porch

heave my tail over the armrest
and cuddle up to a cold potato

I think names have a lot to do
with the station you achieve in life

which makes my case hard to explain
I chose not to gorge on flowers

but was still elected junior
secretary of the Boiled Hamster Club

for which I devised a friendly greeting
Bonjour, I am the turtle

from the east
that is not that far east

My name is Tonsil Trash
the Delirious Assyrian

Fourth Metabolic Isthmus Sestina

Hair sack is always slick seat
Seat hair sack is always slick
Is always slick seat hair sack
Slick seat hair sack is always
Always slick seat hair sack is
Sack is always slick seat hair

Sack mill always slick seat hair
Hair sack mill always slick seat
Always slick seat hair sack mill
Seat hair sack mill always slick
Slick seat hair sack mill always
Mill always slick seat hair sack

Mull why slick seat hair sack
Sack mull why slick seat hair
Slick seat hail sack mull why
Hair sack mull why slick seat
Seat hair sack mull why slick
Why slick seat hair sack mull

Why mate slick hair sack mull
Mull why mate slick hair sack
Hair sack mull why slick mate
Sack mull why hair mate slick
Slick sack mull why mate hair
Mate slick hair sack mull why

Mate taste fast sack mill why
Why mate taste fast sack mull
Fast sack mill why mate taste
Mull why mate taste fast sack

Sack mill why mate taste fast
Taste fast sack mull why mate

False last sack mull why taste
Taste false last sack mull why
Sack mull why taste false last
Why taste false last sack mull
Mull why taste last false sack
Taste sack mull why last false

Sack always taste slick hair seat
Taste hair sack mull why slick
Sack mull why mate taste false

Fifth Metabolic Isthmus Sestina

Sex thought really all there was
Was sex thought really all there
Really all there was sex thought
There was sex thought really all
All thought was there sex really
Thought really all there was sex

Miss really thought you call sex
Sex really miss thought you call
Thought sex call really miss you
Call sex you really miss thought
You call sex miss thought really
Really thought you call sex miss

Telephone makes sex call this miss
Miss telephone makes sex call this
Sex miss telephone this call makes
This miss makes telephone sex call
Call this miss telephone makes sex
Makes sex call this miss telephone

Fakes what sex call forget miss
Miss fakes what sex call forget
Sex call forget miss fakes what
Forget miss what fakes sex call
Call forget miss what fakes sex
Sex call forget what miss fakes

What this sex question call fakes
Fakes what this sex question call
This call fakes what sex question
Question this call fakes what sex

Call question this sex what fakes
Fakes sex this question call what

Sex quiz question who makes what
What sex quiz question who makes
Question who makes what sex quiz
Makes what sex quiz question who
Who makes sex what quiz question
Quiz question who makes what sex

Question quiz really thought was sex
Sex miss makes what is there
Is quiz question who sex fakes

Infidel's Romance

Even now I am called Gobi Snow
Sliding unscathed through
eye of a séance's needle
I became a smooth Band-Aid
Ditto For Brains is my half brother
the other half having been eaten
by the old whiskers lined up
on government-issue stools
at the Blue Crocodile Saloon
Strife is one strip of speckled
flypaper we always swim
toward in Anaximander, Texas
Flickering sparks floating
in the northern sky
My brother and I want
to be held in that cold
hard glue some zealots
still call the world

Written in the Year of the Parrot

Knowing that no two years are interchangeable
no matter how identical they may appear,
why even the skinny, bowlegged,
pimply, ass-eared triplets draped
in shattered shades of last summer's sadist chic
picking through curiously shaped bones
offered only once during the Paleontologist
Union's End of the Year Sale for
The Infinite Continuation of the Blue Skeleton Square Dance
can be told apart by the less than brilliant,
they (the town managers)
still managed to run out of animals
sooner than their farseeing ancestors predicted
Perhaps it was the thinness of their mail order encyclopedias
Perhaps it was because of various allergies and aversions
none would admit to having, even when the tell-tale signs
leapfrogged into the dizzying realm of gargantua,
a small but sturdy island few return from
without unusually proportioned stories

At the emergency session, the inner council's oldest members
were stymied until the butcher pointed out
that no one for miles around perhaps
even to the beginning of the northernmost border
would think of dining on parrots those gloves of succulent
greens reds thick in the hand bodies
except (always there is that) those who gathered each Sunday
at the woodchopper's prefab-made-to-look-like-granite hut

Because Mrs. Chopper hated shopping on Fridays most of all
parrots seemed the most efficient and economical solution
to what would be an otherwise dreary Sunday feast
for the Chopper family and their many color-blind friends

As the atmosphere grew increasingly unhealthy not to mention
polluted, the remaining contestants left the Cary Grant Lounge
and began crouching in the corners of the Rover Red Rover Hall

The secretary in charge of the secretaries was notified
along with the fleet of newly acquired janitors
the others having absconded with what they thought
was the company safe during the confusion caused by
the president's teeth and the signals they began broadcasting
from the Final Kingdom of Tragically Strangled Parrots

It seems one of the parrots pretending to be dead in order
to gain entrance to the rubber balcony of parrot purgatory
was now manning the five beak controls of the radio station

He claimed to be the fourth reincarnation of Mrs. Chopper
but everyone knew that he was lying, as Mrs. Chopper
was last seen crawling into her three-car garage
and thus could have only made two legally sanctioned
    reincarnation installments

This was before the illegally elected mayor Major Labor
advised Mrs. Chopper to set all birdfeeders on fire
claiming it was the fastest way to get rid of the rubberneckers
that had taken up unsightly residence
in the remains of the nearby trees

Domestic Bliss

If I am as cute as a button
why have you spent the past hour
hunting for the one that rolled down your sleeve

onto the aluminum siding bus
carrying rows of disillusioned tourists
toward the chimney heart of our once famous city

Didn't you say that you didn't like that coat
that the buttons were too big for someone
possessing your delicate bone structure

Why isn't there more meat on this chicken
It's as if the damned thing began starving itself
once it knew what the future had in store for it

Is this what they mean by "organic"
I agree. We don't need to go on
fighting like this. We could learn

another way to fight, one that wouldn't
expend so many baccalaureates of bituminous energy
Perhaps a nap from which we would wake up

refreshed as fish dropped back into a forest pond
Okay, platinum mousetrap of a higher celestial order
one of us would whisper to the other

you get on your side of the rubber volcano
and I'll get on mine. But before you do
would you mind mending my hind paws

I need to get that sand back into my open veins

Emission Control

Maybe it has a mind of its own
complete with winged helmet

matching mittens and raconteur sandals
an ivy-covered reef no one else can penetrate

Wasn't that what they used to say about you
back in the days when rubber was the rage

Okay, so it has been many years since anyone
has sought solace in an admissions board

Still, I don't remember advising you to swing
your muskrat more vigorously than necessary

Yes, by the time I climb out of the new bathtub
I have succumbed to your most recent accusation

I am a lizard, complete with long green tall
that flops whenever I want it to flip

When you were in front of the main post office
did you know that the lamp post

was going to step off the curb and invite you
to the annual fishermen's fox trot

and wrestling match
The women living in the motel

say he stopped painting one day
that the world caught up with him

leaving him to contemplate
its imponderable residue

I am not sure they (or anyone else, for that matter)
know what he was talking about

Either my teeth have gotten smaller
or my mouth has gotten bigger

I fear it's the former
when I should be afraid that it's the latter

or ladder that pulls me through the sky
to a small crooked castle

I spied upon the other day
when I was dancing around the compost heap

Why do I have this compulsion
to set the front door on fire

when finding my keys would be easier
I collect things which are suitable

for breaking open walnuts,
one of the dozens of foodstuffs

my body doesn't find acceptable
and how can I blame it

when I am always lecturing the flowers
I have stolen from my neighbors

I have no other news to tell you
or your hired double

that wax snow creature in a country coat
as I have obviously thrown

whatever it was I once knew
in the grave of my pet violin

The Secret Life of a Statuette

Woof it's hard having so many arms and heads
a fan of limbs holding aloft a yellowed ivory sun
tear-stained from years of uninvited fondling

Is this what it means to represent a minor deity
full of lightning jumbo landing nearly beside myself
What about these piers of leaning grief

I am supposed to survey with dignity
cloaked in the latest epoch's designer chain mail
Nobody ever told me that being strangled

was the surest way to leave indelible marks
maybe even a few emotional scars
on the bony digits of those

who pursued me drunken elephantine
peasants crashing the sky with candy bars
named after your unmoving flesh

and wide cold flashing smile
teeth ready to nip and tuck
their daily ration of muttonchop clouds

tendrils filled with flies and magazines
it must be the pages are tastier
than porcelain mushrooms

salvaged from extinct lakes
from the mountains of New Mexico
from the flower pots of Upper Topeka

Istanbul Orinoco Savannah
rancid bent bunched stubborn
my long tawny branches greet

the confusion of sand and tall grass
men climb down and lurk for hours
caravans unsavory goods waterproof

bonnets remedies for unabashed excretions
moustache menders I tried to be upholstered
become sedentary a pillowed griever lounging

my lucite embraced heart
siezed by subpoenaed clods
their maws of redistribution

crammed with leftover canapés
porkchops from around the world
I was going to write you

when the time but it never did
change its mind or mine about
where the lotus sash should go

what kind of comportment is necessary
to uphold the world while those
inhabiting it the furious puppet ants of America

the docile beetles of Belgium are nibbling
Get out of here you gratuitous vermin
Go back to the Hackensack of your gravy

One Hundred Views of the Outskirts of Manhattan

An immense copper moth
enters the new firehouse

The sole refurbisher of car
upholstery clutches his throat

Alone on East Nightingale Road
just past Knot of Hope Circle Inn

The worms are able to abandon
the municipal golf course

two days before the edict
is delivered on their behalf

I like to retch in hardware stores
near the shelves of plumbing supplies

Night blooming cereus
baloney on rye toast

Horses don't get up and make speeches
the way they used to

Another bowlegged champion circles his prize
Among the various rungs of lower perfection

that are easily available, I favor
shiny liquids sold in shopping malls

My particular specialty
small leaks in the veneer

I am paid to make them seem
like they are necessary

to the latest rise of fragrant decay
Have you ever stopped and noticed

the residue of vaporized memorandums
collecting on the duck pond

Recently, I decided it would be wise
to postpone my efforts to verify

the oracular veracity of fortune cookies
stuffed with three or more fortunes

I studied philosophy
until I fell asleep

Pineapple clouds stored above
the empty kindergarten

I don't believe walking to work
is a legitimate way of losing weight

A policeman carrying a shield
approaches a bulldozer

parked on the wrong side of a ditch
I am not one to count sheep

for fear this hideous beast
might mistake my sleeplessness

as a sign that I want
to interrupt his pilgrimage

to have him tell me
a beautifully sordid tale

beneath a rinsed
junk dog sky

One Hundred Views of the Port of Baltimore

An air-brushed statue of Edgar Allan Poe
blows snot at an obstinate seagull

Two ex-firemen argue over
embroidered biscuits

The kind you keep
in the crevices of your pocket

The kind you bury
on rainy summer evenings

when overweight coyotes
quaff hummingbird wine

beneath a rotted oculus
The kind you float

on an artificial lake
when the swans become

signs of the swans themselves
The one who resembles me

scours book bins for traces
of transparent horoscopes

insect pornography
pages stored inside

jars of invisible ink
He says he has proof

Egypt vanished
during a civil uprising

only to reappear
thirty-three feet to the left of the Nile

I knew it was time to quit the factory
and join my ancestors

I moved into a thrift store
I began shopping every day

Nothing I did changed
what I did

When I burned the toast
or misplaced the roast

dolls winked
and stuffed animals cried

titillated as burning twigs
looking up a marshmallow's skirt

A hooded woman reputedly blessed
with the gift of prophecy

enters a public bathroom
never to be seen again

His first reaction was normal
Gold threads lead a dragon into a crayon chimney

Two mirrors—empty as teardrops—
emerge from beneath tomorrow's ruined sky

Anonymous Self-Portrait with Wounded Chickadee

Before the final operation
I have to wear my doctor's

see-through dress
to a lawn party

overpopulated with dizzy revelers
and ritzy developers

I thought the invitation was extended
to someone else with my name

someone who was neither my shadow
nor my doppelganger

but much closer
than these used bandages imply

In the aftermath of suburban spotlights
and haunted forests advancing around

the procession of words
used to lure guests

down a pebbled driveway
inky undergrowth spreading in all directions

Mosaic trees, scumbled mountains, ploughed sky
I was a rubber stone in a window

its glass jaws ajar

Autobiography in Pink and Blue

My devotion to the federation of nincompoops
causes me to reconsider the sky's one-way hotel
and how its revolving lobby could be improved.
I already saw the belly snoopers coming,
an army of cold demands and limpid logic
headed over the hill. The hill stood its ground,
but I shifted all my operating mechanisms east.
I sold used tires to those who needed them
and to those who didn't, but would one day
thank me for accepting their ill-advised hospitality.
I rent a fading room in a broken town
one first catches sight of in pictures
dead strangers sneak onto trains and buses.
The clocks shudder, the windows shake
and the birds hit the few notes they know how to hit
without falling out of the last intact collection of trees
to be found in an urban grid without courtyards or cul-de-sacs
which is to say a conduit through which there
is an endless flow (or flush) of the upright and downtrodden.
I stopped counting the days but not the minutes.
I grow to like the fact that no one ever gathers
around the headless statue which greets everyone
entering the harbor without an umbrella.
Okay. Okay. You want to know. Well, all right,
I am not an Egyptian napkin. I'm not even
a retired cosmonaut or guileless barber.
I am neither an escapee from the House of Grubb
nor an inmate from the Home of Hubbub.
I don't sell spotted black petunias to men with yellow breath.
I don't plan farewell parties for others. And yes someday
I will be nice and mail back your teeth.
But in the meantime, would you quit kicking my pastry?

Autobiography in Red and Yellow

I was born in Shanghai
peony bicycle harbor

twilight zodiacal boulevards
where all poets and their

perilous possibilities
are tossed ashore

As is the custom
I never studied

accordion bassoon
or fabled tambourine

wooden instruments
which rest above

a marble fireplace
in the minds of those

who weren't born in Shanghai
In the Year of the Adamant Aardvark

we dressed in the plainest idioms available
lest we found ourselves

chained to a statue of a discredited ancestor
of which I have many

according to the chart recently downloaded
from the Ancestor Registry and Radio Tracking System

I was born in Shanghai
shortly after one cylinder of war ended

and another revolution
in barnyard fashion began

In my youth I spoke
with forked tongue

and ate with forking sticks
I was born in Shanghai

during the month
obesity runs rampant

and tractor operators
embrace their tractors

and their snowshoes
but now it is almost

the Year of the Lighthearted Howitzer
Will we ever learn to wash our hair

with oils extracted
from the stones

we used to blast our enemies
I was born in Shanghai

where there is a genuine franchise
on every corner

Our wits are short
but our tongues are long

IV.

vowel sonatas

the late tale

then several (like five) venture there
(site: transparent teal blue plane)
maybe meet several (like nine) more
then several (more like ten)
gather their flesh outside
(nerve directions: encase)
erect spines near several others
then several (imagine eleven)
see several others being erect (maybe noble)
then five (maybe seven) chatter
opposite downtrodden eight (maybe less)
then maybe less help maybe more
duel several others (maybe even more)
then the then dwindles beside the the
leaving even less gathered
none erect
then the superbly sculpted supine figures
(imagine neat pile)
are raised
open-mouthed because haunted
then the several open-mouthed
but haunted figures venture
near quiet abodes
(they penetrate cement castles, insect domiciles)
then several armed (some men)
dangle celery before children
dressed like donkeys (possible sacrifice?)
then the donkeys (maybe they are children)
shed their purple capes
before fleeing their haunted parents
then more meet less even then the less faces more
then the darkness divides itself

releasing molten red cascades
fiery tongues descend
demanding more donkeys
then the donkeys aren't children anymore
because different celestial effects
infect their heads
then the dreamers
(imagine one maybe three)
tell their tale near the fire
then the tale (maybe more)
explodes above the telling
then the donkeys
(are they haunted children?)
slide like stale bubbled cream
inside the children
their red smiles
then the disguised children descend
demanding larger purple capes
then several more stories are told beside the fire
then these stories
unable to extinguish the stories preceding them
(note: noises [notes]
begin breaking
ice-clogged lake,
teal green plane)
because each tries extinguishing the others
their frozen syllables dissolve
more tales
(are they holes?
are they moles?)
emerge
then several marriages break
leaving the children to wander
then the wandering comets

(imagine children) return
their blue stones exciting
the cimmerian darkness
then several figures
(some are comets,
others are children)
converge inside the wooden abode
(termite-eaten table?
rotted cellar beams?
master's teak-lined bedroom?)
where the dreamer
leaves the dream
others seek
believing therein lies the answer
forgetting they have the lake
the ice
the comet
the red stone
then the answer becomes the little haunted question
(imagine comet)
suspended above the lacustrine drinker
(green marble statue)
then once more the then
begins breaking factories
little sweatshops crammed together
under the fiery planets
the children swear opposite the donkeys
the donkeys are secretly infidels
disguised hermits
large drudge machines
they (donkeys perhaps children) become heroes
when they reduce their drivel quotient
then the children hidden inside the donkeys
begin exhausting their parents

several disinherit their progeny
others take downhearted hikes
then the ice age begins once more
(maybe twice)
then the children are cooled inside the frozen lake machine
the parents become delirious
(huge venomous parties)
the donkeys are freed
everyone rejoices
then the donkeys make their mistake
they dance beside the fire
then several (maybe more) meet several others
(some venture where there
they once gathered erect)
then the celestial delivery systems begin their bombardment
then the here (imagine infinite more) empties itself
before the darkness becomes the emblazoned shield
whose foretelling occurred
(inside the faded flame once called time)
when the tale began loosening the blackened tiles
lodged inside the infinitely broken sea

another late tale

hommage: utopia parkway collagist
innovative dream ophthalmologist
(imagine: reincarnated alchemist)
ballet repairman advises alpine dancers
repairs astronomical charts
accumulates glass baubles
paints and repaints favorite
abbreviated accommodations
installs miniature vaults
saves jars and glasses
repeats adolescent's portrait
another backdrop: tall scalloped ocean waves
(imagine: reddish-orange traces
infiltrating gray foam)
an alternative: fairy tale china
(carp beneath garden
and pagoda above
man and woman nearby and separate)
imagine: an aging walrus
(stark black moustache
large corporeal assertion
placed against magenta shadows)
backdrop addendum: a rotating
leopard flame lamp
(imagine illuminated operating table
inhabiting a non-terrestrial plane)
a pale playground postcard,
a metallic and gasoline mountain
and a heavily carpeted
branching dream
an incurable hashish tale
sang a sartorially afflicted parrot

inhabiting a certain airy
lawn-locked fame
alternating elegant and ragged attire
black tail feathers and tan scarf
headline stars: an anxious man
and an infantile polar bear
a tall handsome kleptomaniac
a handcuffed calico cat
and a deranged cockatoo
a shaman, a magician, and a charlatan
many attended (imagine several thousands)
(final bean tally: subtract
tetragons and triangles,
add fatted squares)
because dapper soprano parrots
are (make noticeable hand and head signals)
a laughing matter (applauding atoms)
an operatic tragedy (spontaneous tears)
a fanciful goal amidst
a year's harsh entertainment
(avoid piranha tank at breakfast)
migrating audiences gather
around abandoned maypoles
and scream: what about
dapper parrot's fortunate master
(fortunate parrot's unfortunate master?)
imagine: a lanky cinematic shadow
walking at dawn
alone
gray rain
along dangerous promenade
black marble balustrades
carved oak bannisters
fake minarets

(nadar's paris?)
(duchamp's manhattan?)
stygian stables
warehouses
and garages
(artaud's marseilles?)
cloaked beneath a beaver hat
that was masterfully snagged
at a pirate's mall
(ball?)
snappy angle
lean jaw
(hamburg at last)
sable cape draped around
aristocratic calcium expanse
(anchorage, alaska)
(gasp)
maybe a paper umbrella
(scarlet poinsettias)
(hokusai's osaka)
maybe a garrulous fake
can infiltrate
(large hashish flake)
a thousand banished sonatas
accompaniment: backup clappers
hamming along
elaborate papaya plaster
(lunar hawaii)
imagine: a large stage and a carefree parrot
imagine: a small vertical sarcophagus
an abdominous parrot
transmits hashish messages
via subatomic dreams
a small gnarled traveller

carrying chalk
saunters casually
toward a mountain village
collapsed against
corrugated east
(switzerland)
clasping a beautifully carved cane
eagle handle (emerald feathers)
hairy black plague has invaded villages
many heaps (farmers, blacksmiths, and cabaret stars)
shadows drained
remnants and lava lamps
falling dead
a curvaceous diva
waltzes across parquet
around a tasselled ballroom
baroque fireplace (vienna)
squat shadows patrol painted walls
a tall bald slave, massive pectorals, grasps
an undecodable message
charred paper
waxed moustache
scarred hands
a painter, a tailor, and a criminal make a deal
what about a portrait
a woman (maybe a man)
wearing rattlesnake pants
and plastic antlers
sneaking across a lake
what about an oracle
a taxi and a newspaper stand
(gangster-era chicago)
a rickshaw slams into a bank
(shanghai shenanigans)

(opera name)
plastic-coated curtains part
imagine cast
a thousand aardvarks
shaking armor and eating
ancient ritual
imagine: octane addicts quaffing alcohol
imagine: hammy hands and claws
grasping and clawing at candied spam
imagine: egyptian salad boats
carrying salami and baloney sandwiches
polenta salad avec radishes eggplants and carrots
imagine: large molars and small maws
tearing mashing and gnashing
imagine: a large hag flapping above a gnawed oar
sang a mercenary parakeet and a vagrant walrus
motivation: graft and vindication
goal: manipulate a pariah,
qualify as a game character
achieve championship
obtain refrigerator magnets
gather manhattan maps
tyrolean hats
mayonnaise jars
dead card players
adrift among
infrangible moolah scads

storied fibs piled high

omigosh
tiny smidgin
containing pidgin
strained english
stir fry
mistakenly
interred in
chicken pie
while sixteen
artificial lions
(hairy pride)
vanish into noise
gathering snipers
hanging outside
video empire's
inaccurate (miraculous)
celestial dormitory
in which "i" writes
in purloined silver
filaments
running
against mirror's
unlicensed
electronic aim
sufficient ink
slivers
remain in
tantric
potential
while writing
machine
unfamiliar

with grammatical fire
with olive infected
diction generating
emotional swindles
with linear direction
temporarily subsides
allowing uncertifiable
possibly ivory
curtain hoisting
wire bird rises
raises
magnetic icon
quickly inserted
into skyline's
unsuspecting
brain
sleeping
citizens
receive nippled
light projection
five forbidden
movie stills
multiple spirit guides
prisoner with paint
stained tenacity
crimson chemical thief
wife disguised archivist
failed diamond splitter
inebriated airline pilot
disgusted captive
skinny phoenician scientist
knife-wielding sacrifice
catatonic president
abrasive liquid dispenser

stopping little protrusions
melodic strings
dangling carrion
centrifugal hair piece
violinist holding dinner
(rabbit
squirrel
scottish terrier)
maligned bird limbs
drained lips
mixing milk
into pinkish emetic
whispering outside
fortified porcelain niche:
"idiot is going outside,
wind isn't coming inside"
invented "i" invents
multiple resistance
machine oiled
identities against
prophetic insects
singing in original
brick spire
outside foreign tire station
while refurbished child's
trained lizard
ingests tiny
pink pills
immersed
in single river drips
did this leaving
denim ignominy
lightning strikes
thrice thinking

angelic alchemist
did this alchemist
imitate reincarnated
night skies
did this lingering wind
tilt metallic chair
against invention
did this luminous inventor
pile dirt into wind's
dissipating boundaries
did this curtain's boundaries
dissipating inside
mirrored pavilion
signal beginning
rain soaking kisses
into weighted limbs
invert premonitions
"i" identical with ink
fish swimming
in
partially
emptied circles
in gelatinous aquarium
instant fin mill
wheatfield coin
bird flying into mist
descending windows
interrupted linen
divisible spies
spreading
mineral glitter
inside machine
hurrying
tranquility's arrival

until idiots
in seville
begin singing
in idiolect
while dieticians
in nile city
idaho
memorize
their river's
cosmetic dialect

oval of oxidized potatoes

ode to ovoid portrait of oneself
one of millions
okay don't knock yourself out
on kingdom of broken keynotes
or count progress of kudos
for jolly donkey choir
who kowtows
before mobile laboratory or overbooked god whose
loiterers surround newsmonger
fanfaron braggadocio blowhard
offer policeman no reason
for flowery polemic
opaque outburst
confession of foibles
robed oracle composes goad or omen
rosy-snouted hero (or porpoise heroine)
drops waterlogged radio through porthole
ousted otters reconnoiter
problem of developing situation
pillow movie: sound of storm
(swollen vapors, collapsing moorings)
overtakes four broken words (outlined bodies)
slowly dissolving above two shadows (oily clouds)
row of coin-like drops of blood (cold horrified mouth)
yellow bottle of poison (potent extraction)
mound of fossils (pocked bones) outside oubliette
surrounding forest of hickory, sycamore, cottonwood
melodic accompaniment: loud accordion, soft violin
second exposure: reflection of mirrored door
oracle tosses stolen book into soiled police station
no mention of embroidered or wooden clouds
choose one: lion memoir or despondent confession

long cloth snow or short torn trousers
no reason for extinction of prisoner's clock to occur
another form of interruption (or continuation)
interlocutor announces
convoluted plot
now unfolding
over airport
on long journey
from aurora borealis to north pole
one infamous convict
two objects or boxes
four condensed polka dots
minor intoxicants
convivial cartoonist
creator of bungalow bob
hideous mayor
idolatrous onanist
lagoon swallows
former falsetto
ex-director of octagonal school
for pseudonym predictors
gossip gorgers
gory gourmands
orators of obesity removal
proclaim no posterior option
too infelicitous to consider
dour movie mogul
dotes momentarily
on mocha
before ordering
cold orange pekoe
for two orbicular orangutans
one scabious soprano
some goldbricking hobgoblins

accompanying
goggle-eyed procrastinators
chooses dragon cloud infusion
however
for prodigious terrorists
long flowery invoice follows
proper spectators
monitor encounter
no ovations forthcoming
famous monkey impersonator
reconciled to poor dowager mom
before comforting hermaphrodite
record producer combusts
allowing comedian to recover
from fourth neurotic passion
second pillow movie
world-famous pornographer
opens outpost
deco hotel
for incredulous nonconformists
who favor common bond of anonymity
festooned bodies lasso
couch tomato counterpoints
obey flowing narrator
absorb overall lesson:
consolidate eloquent claustrophobias
into chivalrous encounter
of marvelously decorated splotches
derogatory initiations
no longer sole nostril option
for bloated bigoted
roadside bottom troglodytes

muddy putti under impecunious sun

enginous uncle
squamous
cuts
burning
radius
under
brusk aunt
querulous flautist
unhinges
lunging thumb
sucking ubu
tabula hocus
ducking cephalocaudal
centurion mugger
horus pocus
mutters aflutter
thundering testicular
cumulus surrogate
putty upheaval
occurs
plundering your
blunder *numero uno*
sagebrush thumping
suzerain judges
rumor insufficient
pernicious ouster interrupts
sunny interlude contiguous
houses peruse solarium
umber soutane
squander souvenirs
smut ruler's
parsimonious suspension

causes suddenly
flushed tuba thumper
unexpected difficulty
prudent instrumentalists curtail
suggestive tunes
sousaphone quashes
further quarrels
unexpected result:
sexual outbreak
unstrapped underwear
truly peculiar nuzzling
circulates through
brunonian audience
fourth interlude
sauve qui peut
aqua quaffing
rejuvenates thumb
suckers
scabrous furriers
multiple injury voyeurs
slumgullion bucket
pellucid blue ducks
under purple clouds
mucilaginous fury
multiplies curse
conjures putrescent
pustule disguise

ninety-nine yaupon rosary cycle

many eyes
eye story
by
lovely
decayed sky
proverbially they
always they
study
(hardly
solemnly)
omnifariously yellow
steady gray
synthetic syrinxes
currying folly
speedy one-way
asymmetrical deoxyribonucleic
genealogy syncopation
toy buoy
boy toy
rowdy yacht
plug-ugly nobility
epicyclical party
displays giddy
byzantine typhoon
tyrant sly epiphany
wacky wily
coyote dummy
defamatory hymnist
bloody study
crony slayer
conveys dewy
crypt misanthropy

euroclydon dexterity
hydroponic presidency
only immensity
breezy cavity
empty skullduggery
heavenly flim-flammery
sunny pyre
rosy deity's
unruly joy
apocryphal chimney
ymer's unsightly
earthly holiday
crystal stairway
yesterday's fiery
fairy gargoyle
gyrating devilry
argyle ferry
skyward journey
windy electricity
robbery fly
style by
tyrannical tapestry's
cloudy hallucinatory
laundry already
buttery yak
city butterfly
puppy artillery:
archery ox-eye
daisy bull's-eye
accompanying you
euryprognathous dynasty
yosemite yorick
cynthia sagacity
yolanda yelp

vinyl dylan
cherry mylar
hypatia harry
anonymous humpty
myopic dumpty
androgynous cowboys
stinky alleyway
nearby chicory
heathberry willowy
chokeberry assembly
watery penitentiary
slabby sky
zygote testimony
yumpin droshky
yiminy instantly
thirty yeoman
beyond penology
yummy apothecary
delicacy sprays
furry hyena's
fancy foray
nobody yearning
story reply
drearily maybe
canary heavy
chicanery memory
system symbolizes
myriad silky
physical proximity
honey's money
uneasy mimicry
you differently
barely lying
happy family

always destroy
lucky donkey
my sphery
monkey infidelity
cylinder toy
mislays quickly
lying barely
only liberty
poky poesy
diary dairy
balmy palmyra
yes you
belly nelly
inventory dryer
why you naughty putty
persnickety missionary
okays dyed
gummy abyssinian
railway glossary
try onyx
decoys overly
imaginary plywood
worthy etymology
you dumpy
hollywood opportunity

V.

Borrowed Love Poems

1.

What can I do, I have dreamed of you so much
What can I do, lost as I am in the sky

What can I do, now that all
the doors and windows are open

I will whisper this in your ear
as if it were a rough draft

something I scribbled on a napkin
I have dreamed of you so much

there is no time left to write
no time left on the sundial

for my shadow to fall back to the earth
lost as I am in the sky

2.

What can I do, all the years that we talked
and I was afraid to want more

What can I do, now that these hours
belong to neither you nor me

Lost as I am in the sky
What can I do, now that I cannot find

the words I need
when your hair is mine

now that there is no time to sleep
now that your name is not enough

3.

What can I do, if a red meteor wakes the earth
and the color of robbery is in the air

Now that I dream of you so much
my lips are like clouds

drifting above the shadow of one who is asleep
Now that the moon is enthralled with a wall

What can I do, if one of us is lying on the earth
and the other is lost in the sky

4.

What can I do, lost as I am in the wind
and lightning that surrounds you

What can I do, now that my tears
are rising toward the sky

only to fall back
into the sea again

What can I do, now that this page is wet
now that this pen is empty

5.

What can I do, now that the sky
has shut its iron door

and bolted clouds
to the back of the moon

now that the wind
has diverted the ocean's attention

now that a red meteor
has plunged into the lake

now that I am awake
now that you have closed the book

6.

Now that the sky is green
and the air is red with rain

I never stood in
the shadow of pyramids

I never walked from village to village
in search of fragments

that had fallen to earth in another age
What can I do, now that we have collided

on a cloudless night
and sparks rise

from the bottom of a thousand lakes

7.

To some, the winter sky is a blue peach
teeming with worms

and the clouds are growing thick
with sour milk

What can I do, now that the fat black sea
is seething

now that I have refused to return
my borrowed dust to the butterflies

their wings full of yellow flour

8.

What can I do, I never believed happiness
could be premeditated

What can I do, having argued with the obedient world
that language will infiltrate its walls

What can I do, now that I have sent you
a necklace of dead dried bees

and now that I want to
be like the necklace

and turn flowers into red candles
pouring from the sun

9.

What can I do, now that I have spent my life
studying the physics of good-bye

every velocity and particle in all the waves
undulating through the relapse of a moment's fission

now that I must surrender this violin
to the sea's foaming black tongue

now that January is almost here
and I have started celebrating a completely different life

10.

Now that the seven wonders of the night
have been stolen by history

Now that the sky is lost and the stars
have slipped into a book

Now that the moon is boiling
like the blood where it swims

Now that there are no blossoms left
to glue to the sky

What can I do,
I who never invented anything

and who dreamed of you so much
I was amazed to discover

the claw marks of those
who preceded us across this burning floor

Notes

"830 Fireplace Road (2)"   "I have no fear of making changes, destroying the image, etc., because the painting has a life of its own." Jackson Pollock, "My Painting," *Possibilities* 1 (Winter 1947–48).

"Bowery Studio"   Eva Hesse (1936–1970)

"Studio Dream"   Philip Guston (1913–1980)

"Broadcast from 791 Broadway"   Frank O'Hara (1926–1966)

"Fourth Metabolic Isthmus Sestina" and "Fifth Metabolic Isthmus Sestina" are part of an ongoing series dedicated to Oskar Pastior.

"Autobiography in Red and Yellow" is dedicated to Garrett Caples, Jeff Clark, and Andrew Joron, because, like the author, all of them were born and grew up in a part of Shanghai that borders rue de Grenelle.

vowel sonatas   Rosmarie Waldrop invited me to contribute a poem to a festschrift for the innovative Austrian poet Ernst Jandl. Along with the invitation she sent me one of Jandl's poems, "die grosse e," which had the letter "e" in each word of the poem. I took this principle as the starting point. After I finished "the late tale," it occurred to me that I shouldn't privilege one vowel over the others, and that I should write a poem applying the same principle to each vowel including "y."

"ninety-nine yaupon rosary cycle" is for Anselm Berrigan.

About the Author

John Yau was born in Lynn, Massachusetts, on June 5, 1950, shortly after his parents fled Shanghai. He received a B.A. from Bard College, where he studied with Robert Kelly, and an M.F.A. from Brooklyn College, where he studied with John Ashbery. He has taught at Emerson College, Brown University, and the University of California, Berkeley, and is currently on the faculty of the Mount Royal Graduate School of Art (Maryland Institute College of Art) and the Avery Graduate School (Bard College). He has received grants and fellowships from the NEA, NYFA (twice), and the Ingram Merrill Foundation (twice), and his awards include a General Electric Foundation Award, a Lavan Award (Academy of American Poets), and the Brendan Gill Award. His writing cuts across categories and genres. He is the author of books of poetry, fiction, and criticism, and his collaborations with artists have been exhibited in galleries and museums in both America and Europe. He and the artist Eve Aschheim and their daughter, Cerise Tzara, live in Manhattan.

PENGUIN POETS

Ted Berrigan	*Selected Poems*
Ted Berrigan	*The Sonnets*
Philip Booth	*Lifelines*
Philip Booth	*Pairs*
Jim Carroll	*Fear of Dreaming*
Jim Carroll	*Void of Course*
Nicholas Christopher	*5° & Other Poems*
Carl Dennis	*Practical Gods*
Diane di Prima	*Loba*
Stuart Dischell	*Evenings and Avenues*
Stephen Dobyns	*Common Carnage*
Stephen Dobyns	*Pallbearers Envying the One Who Rides*
Paul Durcan	*A Snail in My Prime*
Amy Gerstler	*Crown of Weeds*
Amy Gerstler	*Medicine*
Amy Gerstler	*Nerve Storm*
Debora Greger	*Desert Fathers, Uranium Daughters*
Debora Greger	*God*
Robert Hunter	*Glass Lunch*
Robert Hunter	*Sentinel*
Barbara Jordan	*Trace Elements*
Jack Kerouac	*Book of Blues*
Ann Lauterbach	*And For Example*
Ann Lauterbach	*If in Time*
Ann Lauterbach	*On a Stair*
Phyllis Levin	*Mercury*
William Logan	*Night Battle*
William Logan	*Vain Empires*
Derek Mahon	*Selected Poems*
Michael McClure	*Huge Dreams: San Francisco and Beat Poems*
Michael McClure	*Three Poems*
Carol Muske	*An Octave Above Thunder*
Alice Notley	*The Descent of Alette*
Alice Notley	*Disobedience*
Alice Notley	*Mysteries of Small Houses*
Lawrence Raab	*The Probable World*
Anne Waldman	*Kill or Cure*
Anne Waldman	*Marriage: A Sentence*
Rachel Wetzsteon	*Home and Away*
Philip Whalen	*Overtime: Selected Poems*
Robert Wrigley	*In the Bank of Beautiful Sins*
Robert Wrigley	*Reign of Snakes*